Beginning Jazz

Seven Easy Solos

By

Geoff Haydon

Ham and Eggs
Jazz It Up
Leisure Time
A Rainy Day
Sunny Day
Blues Mystery
Savannah Rag

Tracks 1, 2, 3, 4

Ham and Eggs

Rock Beat - even eighths (M.M. ♩ = c. 110)

Geoff Haydon

4

Tracks 5, 6, 7, 8

Jazz It Up

Geoff Haydon

Leisure Time

Tracks 9, 10, 11, 12

Geoff Haydon

A Rainy Day

Tracks 13, 14, 15, 16

Geoff Haydon

Slowly ♩ = 72

Sunny Day

Easy Swing (M.M. ♩ = c. 110)

Geoff Haydon

Blues Mystery

Tracks 21, 22, 23 24

Geoff Haydon

Improvise using these tones
from the C Blues scale

16

Improvise using these tones
from the C Blues scale

2409

Savannah Rag

Geoff Haydon

Moderato ♩ = c. 126